CONTENTS

INTRODUCTION 3

The Rise of Entrepreneurship 6

Impact of Crises 8

The Idea of Collective Efforts 14

Practical Experience and Observations 18

Prospects for Implementing the Idea 20

Development of a SaaS Solution 24

CONCLUSION 35

INTRODUCTION

The idea I will share with you in this book first came to me in 2018. It struck me on my way from Moscow to Tver to visit my parents while I was mentally summing up the results of the outgoing year and gradually planning the next one. You know, it's good to think while on the road if you don't focus on things like music or phone calls. I was driving my not-so-new, but personally purchased from an official dealer car. Thoughts about my past career as a marketing specialist for car dealers, my first entrepreneurial experiences with them, and client orders were swirling in my head.

"This is how life turned out — I was a dealer's client, now dealers are my clients... Funny how it worked out...

How fortunate with those social media videos we made for the client on our own initiative for free... The client appreciated it, immediately thanked us, and boasted to his colleagues, marketers of other car dealers. They wanted the same videos with their logos and contacts, and within fifteen minutes, our messengers were literally bursting. So we managed to earn a little on our philanthropy. Wow! Do good deeds and you will be rewarded..."

All these thoughts led me to reflect on topics of interactions — communications, mutual assistance, alliances, and, on the contrary, envy.

"Why did she share the video with others? Just to show off, why not... And the same promotional material was suitable for all these dealers! Logically, they are not competitors because they operate in different regions... Then why don't they always do this? Why reinvent the wheel if someone has already done it somewhere...

Surely they do this, but in some small groups - among those who are especially close to each other, with whom they communicate more often. And most likely by some completely random circumstances... I don't remember any special barter platforms when I worked in marketing. Maybe something has changed since then..."

These dialogues with myself in my head eventually made me ask my clients where and how they communicate with each other, with colleagues, so to speak, how often they interact, who is the initiator, and how this is organized. It turned out that it all boils down to sheer randomness, and more often such communication happens during annual conferences for specialists for training, motivation, and other team-building practices from vendors[1].

It is hardly possible to create an effective community of representatives of the dealer network solely through conferences. In my opinion, attempts to create it cannot be successful without a system based on regular interaction. Cultural events in a voluntary format are not enough; there must be a specific measurable profit for everyone. Measurable and fair.

The vendors themselves cannot organize the work of their networks in this way for two main reasons, as it seems to me.

The first reason is management strategy. The fear of losing control over the work of individual dealers, the entire network as a whole, and the unified direction of federal advertising campaigns carefully thought out and implemented by them and their expensive advertising contractors. Vendors are not interested in giving their dealers a tool for real effective interaction among themselves and dissipating their efforts in building centralized advertising and image campaigns because they fear harming what they have already invested in and continue to do according to their marketing strategies for the coming years. Simply put, it would contradict their already established network management system. It is much safer and easier to manage through the "dealer-vendor" system rather than "dealer-dealer".

The second reason is the multibrand nature of car dealers. Partly stems from the first reason. The same dealer can have more than one or even ten car dealerships and be not just a company but an entire business group with interests in selling cars and other automotive brands. Creating convenient tools for dealer interaction means creating conditions for promoting other brands too, which logically contradicts common business practices. This would set a trend, leading to the emergence of similar products from other vendors and, over time, cross-platform solutions from independent parties. Thus, initially, this is a task rather for third parties, such

---

1 They are distributors, factories or suppliers, depending on the specific situation with the terms of supply or the wishes of the vendors themselves to call themselves one way or another.

as IT companies, which cannot and should not be part of the strategy of a single vendor.

Thus, one way or another, the vendor is not interested in changing its management system, and as a result, all assistance boils down to providing ready-made (in the vendor's opinion, but often needing improvement or creating other materials based on them) advertising materials and standards for conducting promotional events. Essentially, controlling dealers. Moreover, the independent creativity of dealers is often not welcomed or even punished — in my practice as a marketer with seven car brands, it was exactly like this. Dealers are required to use predominantly the promotional and image materials provided to them by the vendor through a special dealer portal. There are many opinions and debates in marketing regarding the effectiveness of PIM and strategies, so it has happened that many marketers prefer to create and use their materials, sometimes even secretly from the vendor.

In addition to the absence of an existing solution for joint work, exchange of practices, and PIM, there is an internal factor — the lack of motivation among dealers themselves to do this. There is no specialized tool that would organize such processes, track the fairness of compensation and the value of each person's contribution to the common cause. The logic here is this — I will share something and in return, I will get something less valuable or nothing at all. Better we do everything ourselves the old-fashioned way…

Realizing all this, I saw unique opportunities and understood what I want to do in the near future.

THE RISE OF ENTREPRENEURSHIP

You have undoubtedly noticed how dramatically the world around us has changed in the 21st century. With the advent of the internet, social media, YouTube, and countless online courses, humanity has gained numerous opportunities to earn money. Many new business niches have opened the way to financial prosperity for young and enterprising people.

In the past, our parents and grandparents could, at best, work in a factory, a store, or a market (often difficult to reach). Today, we have an endless number of bloggers, various online stores, marketplaces, dropshipping businesses, startup incubators, and info businesses around every corner. Trade, IT, neural networks... The degree and pace of business changes today are astonishing — approximately every five years, one trend is replaced by another.

Every second person thinks about starting their own business, every third has already tried to start one, and every tenth is already an entrepreneur to some extent. The logic is understandable: why go to work every day, labor from nine to six, and follow the orders of some boss? Over the past two decades, the number of people who have become the authors of their destinies has increased significantly, and this trend continues to gain momentum.

The modern world provides unprecedented opportunities for self-realization. In the era of the internet, where access to information and resources has become incredibly simple, anyone can start their own business. You can begin your journey with small steps: create a blog, open an online store, or start offering services online. This does not require significant initial capital investments or connections, which opens the doors to the world of entrepreneurship for people of all backgrounds, regardless of their initial circumstances.

New technologies and platforms allow businesses to start with minimal costs and maximum flexibility. Online platforms such as Shopify for online stores, YouTube and Spotify for video content, and social networks for promoting services significantly simplify market entry. Dropshipping, for example, allows selling goods without the need to store and manage logistics. Startup incubators provide young entrepreneurs with not only funding but also mentorship, significantly increasing their chances of success.

Furthermore, the rise of freelancing and remote work allows for the simultaneous management of multiple projects, testing different ideas, and choosing the most successful directions. This is a time of experiments and innovations when everyone can find their niche and achieve success.

Despite all these opportunities, the market is becoming increasingly competitive. Not every business withstands the test of time, and many startups close within the first year of their existence. This creates additional incentives for entrepreneurs to constantly learn, adapt, and improve their skills to fight for their place in the sun.

Today, there are numerous training courses for both personal growth and specialized ones aimed at acquiring specific skills in promotion, client acquisition, and establishing internal processes. However, even these opportunities are becoming insufficient as the world does not stand still. Despite the abundance of opportunities to invest in oneself or the promotion of one's product, the cost remains high and often unattainable for most starting entrepreneurs and small businesses.

The same can be said about the advertising market. As competition increases, so do the prices for promoting goods and services. A striking example of this is contextual advertising in search engines. At some point, the cost of attracting a customer through this advertising channel in the market of entrance and interior doors rose so much that it bordered on the margin percentage of these types of goods, making it very conditional to promote there.

With the development of the market, survival in it becomes only more difficult. Modern business realities require not only initiative and courage but also flexibility, the ability to quickly respond to changes, and the use of new technologies and approaches. Those who can quickly adapt and find unconventional solutions have the best chances of success in these dynamic times.

THE IMPACT OF CRISES

Alongside the growth of entrepreneurial activity, the economies of countries continue to expand, creating new jobs and improving the accessibility of goods. With the increase in consumer demand, the need for production also rises: sold goods need to be transported, vehicles need to be fueled, and to support the operation of billions of computers and servers, more stations and substations are required. Gradually, this leads to the growth of resource accessibility issues.

As the economy grows, so do the scales of industrial production. Vehicles become an integral part of our daily lives: they deliver products to stores, goods to warehouses, and parcels to our homes. In my childhood, not every family owned a car, but today, having multiple cars in a family is a common occurrence. All these vehicles require fuel, and the demand for it only increases each day. Computers and servers, which form the basis of our digital infrastructure, also require energy for uninterrupted operation. New stations and substations must meet this demand, providing energy to cities and enterprises.

Simultaneously, the daily needs of the population also demand resources. Bloggers need outlets to create content, and their subscribers need them to consume it. This creates additional pressure on energy systems. More and more people are engaging in the digital economy, and this requires even more energy.

All these changes lead us to today's crucial topic of resource sources. The world is not standing still, and our demand for energy and materials constantly grows. At the same time, fossil fuel reserves are not infinite, and their extraction causes significant harm to the environment. It is customary for us, humans, that authorities do not rush to raise the issue of climate change, but an attentive observer can notice natural disasters happening almost all over the world. Additionally, statements[2] by

---

2 A statement on climate change and the urgent need for action, along with an address by a scientist to the presidents of the USA, China, and Russia, was published on August 14, 2023, on the personal website and YouTube channel of Dr. A. Egon Cholakian.

renowned scientists and studies[3] published in Nature Communications at least make one think about it.

Today, humanity is faced with the necessity of seeking new sources of energy and ways to utilize them. The development of economies and technologies presents us with new challenges. To maintain a balance between growth and sustainable development, we must pay attention to the availability and rational use of resources. This issue is becoming increasingly relevant, requiring innovative solutions and global cooperation.

To sustain current growth rates and ensure stability, sustainable and rational use of natural resources is essential. The topics of ecology, the transition to electric vehicles, and the increasing demand for energy are being raised more frequently around the world. And these are not just discussions — these changes are already happening today. Their significance is confirmed by the laws adopted in various countries and states regarding the transition to electric vehicles.

For example, California[4] and Denmark[5] plan to transition to the sale of new cars with electric engines by 2030. This is not just an economic necessity in the context of growing industrial needs but rather a political step towards addressing environmental pollution issues and improving the quality of life for citizens in these countries.

In 2023, a detailed discussion on transitioning to clean energy sources took place at the annual Edison Electric Institute (EEI)[6] forum. The discussion, led by Elon Musk and Edison Electric Institute President Pedro J. Pizarro, thoroughly examined the prospects for the development of renewable energy.

---

3 According to a study, the Gulf Stream could cease to exist at any moment between 2025 and 2095. Experts have described the potential consequences as climate chaos.

4 The state of California (USA) plans to completely transition to the sale of new cars with electric engines by 2030.

5 Denmark plans to have 775,000 electric or hybrid vehicles on the road by 2030, which is one-third of all cars in the country as of 2024.

6 The Edison Electric Institute (EEI) is an association representing all U.S. investor-owned companies involved in the generation and distribution of electricity.

Elon Musk, known for his active stance on sustainability and innovative energy projects, emphasized the importance of investing in solar and wind energy. He noted that energy production and storage technologies have significantly advanced, making the transition to renewable sources not only possible but also economically beneficial. Musk highlighted Tesla's projects in creating battery systems that can efficiently store energy, ensuring stable power supply even during periods of low renewable energy production.

Pedro J. Pizarro, in turn, underscored the role that large energy companies play in this transition. He pointed out that the electric industry is on the brink of significant changes, and sustainable energy production should become a priority for all market participants. Pizarro also highlighted the importance of government support and regulatory frameworks that can accelerate the adoption of clean technologies.

Both leaders agreed that the transition to renewable energy sources requires a comprehensive approach, including technological innovations, infrastructure changes, and cooperation between the private and public sectors. They discussed possible strategies for overcoming obstacles such as the high initial investment costs and the need to modernize existing power grids.

The discussions held by Musk and Pizarro highlighted the necessity of collective efforts and innovative solutions to achieve global energy and environmental goals.

Modern technologies require new approaches to resource utilization, and it is crucial to understand that economic development inevitably demands innovation. For example, the extraction of oil and gas, as well as other minerals, leads to significant carbon dioxide emissions and environmental disasters. These processes not only harm the environment but also have a cumulative effect, negatively impacting the global climate. The solution to these problems has been found in renewable energy sources, and the rational use of natural resources is becoming an integral part of the global strategy for sustainable development.

> ## Economic development inevitably demands innovation

In my opinion, these same principles of rational resource use should be applied in business. The issue of resource accessibility for small businesses is becoming increasingly relevant, requiring new approaches and solutions on a global level. Innovations in the rational use of such valuable existing resources will become a key factor in sustainable business development in the coming decades. For small businesses, this can be achieved by using renewable technologies in managing their processes. This will allow for more efficient use of available resources and reduce financial costs.

The key to implementing this idea in this field will be the methodologies on which new business processes are based. These methodologies involve the exchange of experiences, resources, and innovations between enterprises.

Business, technology, climate... Let me explain what these lessons in natural science have to do with the topic of business.

Economic development inevitably requires the advancement of technology, and these, in turn, must be safe for us. Here, perhaps, the most illustrative example is the digging of quarries, the extraction of oil, gas, marble, gold, and other minerals from the earth, and the resulting widespread soil collapses, sometimes taking many lives. Carbon dioxide emissions into the atmosphere amount to hundreds of millions of tons annually. The harmful impact on the global climate also arises from the lack of a culture of waste recycling, particularly plastic, which clogs the world's water bodies and affects fauna and wildlife. Like any destructive phenomenon, this has a cumulative effect.

Similarly, the scale of consumption affects the entrepreneurial ecosystem; irrational use of resources here already has a similar effect. If we believe the statistics on the number of people wanting to start their own business in Russia, we see a grim picture. In 2016, 34% of people wanted to start their own business, but by 2022, this number had dropped to

23%. There is an outflow of those wishing to have their own business, and this is akin to the climate crisis of modern entrepreneurship, requiring innovative solutions. These solutions lie in new sources of resources and their more efficient use. We will inevitably have to come to this.

On one hand, the decrease in the number of aspiring entrepreneurs indicates growing risks and difficulties faced by novice businessmen and the small business segment as a whole. Bureaucratic obstacles, high taxes, stiff competition, and the need for significant initial investments can deter many. In such a situation, the decrease in the number of entrepreneurs seems like a worrying signal indicating a worsening business climate. However, on the other hand, it can also mean an increase in the quality of businesses. People are becoming more cautious and thoughtful in their decisions. Those who decide to start their own business do so more deliberately, carefully assessing risks and opportunities. They enter the business with a clearer plan and understanding of what is needed for success. This can lead to the emergence of more sustainable and viable companies capable of withstanding competition and handling crises.

Moreover, the market itself can stimulate more rational resource distribution. The fewer people strive to enter business, the more opportunities existing companies can get for growth and development. For example, in retail, a decrease in new market entrants can lead to less competition for consumers. This allows existing companies to strengthen their positions, increase market share, and invest more resources in innovation and improving service quality. It is important to note that the decrease in new entrepreneurs may be a temporary phenomenon. With the advent of new technologies and opportunities, the number of people willing to try their hand at business may rise again. In my opinion, it is crucial to create favorable conditions for this growth by ensuring access to knowledge, support, and resources.

"Someone has to work!" — a reader might justly note. Why is it necessary to have your own business when there are job market opportunities for seekers?

The author responds. Besides the comparative abundance of options in today's job market, there are also technological trends such as optimization, automation, robotics, and the development of artificial intelligence (AI). The noticeable buzz in this area was caused by the leap in neural network development and their widespread application in recent years. People have started talking about the inevitable loss of jobs in entire industries, which, to some extent, is justified. Just look at the example of Amazon's robotic warehouses, where there is not a single person. Today, this is efficient and economically advantageous. Being an entrepreneur is not easy, but it will sharpen your mind, protect you from the consequences of job cuts, and increase your value as a specialist.

One way or another, the market signals the need for adaptation and the search for new solutions, as well as the importance of a rational and sustainable approach to business development. Ultimately, this can lead to a healthier and more stable entrepreneurial ecosystem, capable of effectively meeting challenges and seizing opportunities for growth and prosperity.

THE IDEA OF UNITING EFFORTS

In 2015, while working on the opening of a large mall with an area of about fifty thousand square meters, I first conceived the idea of collectivization in promotion efforts. Even before the official opening, the complex housed over a hundred tenants, each representing a company or a branch of an existing retail chain.

At that time, I was developing policies for advertising campaigns within the premises of the complex, in the surrounding areas, and working on a long-term advertising strategy for the object. Since the efforts of the complex itself were not enough to achieve a quick effect, the tenants independently invested in advertising their new outlets and the new shopping complex. It was then that I first thought about the concept that companies, even those competing with each other in terms of their product range, could be allies, sharing the same goal of attracting traffic and consumer demand, which would subsequently create opportunities for sales. They got the traffic, and from there, it's fair game — whoever has better sales wins.

Captivated by this paradox, I wanted to create such an ecosystem, improve the quality of tenants' sales, and help them train their salespeople to become real managers, rather than the mediocre ones they were at the time. Most salespeople did not react to visitors, mostly sitting on their mobile phones. Today, this might seem strange, but that was the norm back then.

I saw opportunities in this for the mall and suggested to the management to create something like an academy to increase tenants' engagement in their personal development and the overall development of the complex. The format looked

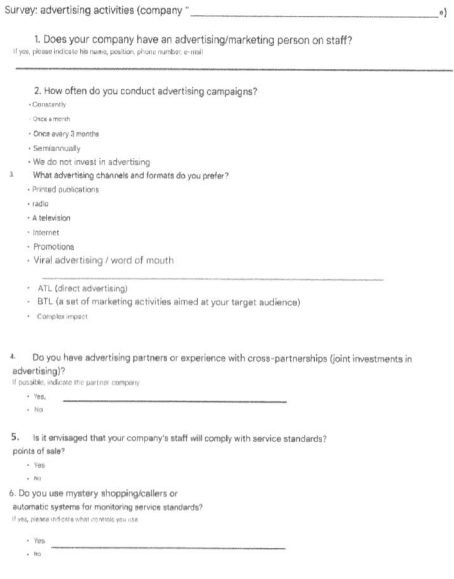

Shopping mall tenant survey form

quite unique and could serve as a unique selling proposition (USP) for potential new tenants of the complex both in this region and elsewhere, if the system were made centralized. Moreover, surveys and live communication showed that most tenants did not have their own advertising specialists but were willing to conduct joint advertising campaigns.

The management predictably did not appreciate the idea. They did not see a direct, clear, and measurable benefit for themselves, traditionally following the well-trodden path. Like the vendors mentioned at the beginning of the narrative, the holding's management viewed their business purely as a business, not as a subject for research and experimentation. An independent third party was needed, a contractor capable of taking on this function. Thus, a unification project was born, resulting in the majority of tenants showing interest and expressing a desire to participate.

At an open conference, 2015

The idea was simple — unite and organize promotion efforts collectively. The main advantage wasn't just this. It lay in collective buying. The advertising budgets in this case would not be small individual amounts but a single unprecedentedly large budget by regional standards, capable of securing significant discounts from agencies, internet portals, TV and radio companies, and other media. To give an example, just a year later, using this same method, I managed to reduce the cost of radio airtime for my client by exactly five times. This was a great example of the effectiveness of joint efforts and the idea of collective action.

Unfortunately, the project did not last long due to my lack of a full-fledged team, necessary resources, and experience working with people at that time. However, there were examples that inspired with their successes.

Perhaps the most striking example for me was the organization AS-NA, which provided opportunities for small retailers to survive during the rise of large chains. This movement became so popular that today its market share, compared to federal pharmacy chains, ranks first in Russia by a significant margin from its nearest competitor. The association continues to grow, serving as a living testament to the effectiveness of collective work. While the model was not historically the first in the world[7], it was the first and most popular in the country. In 2018, there were so many ASNA pharmacies that Yandex and Addreality launched indoor advertising sales in this network. This was the first experience in Russia of using programmatic technologies for indoor advertising. The pharmacy network became an advertising platform... Such was the uniqueness of this experience.

Despite the presence of successful examples, the constant demand for motivating small businesses remains a key factor for their sustainable development. Small enterprises often face a lack of resources and knowledge, highlighting the need for ongoing development of business technologies aimed at increasing their survivability. With extensive experience in this area, we are certainly capable of offering solutions that help entrepreneurs and companies avoid repeating the same mistakes and take advantage of the collective experience already accumulated. It just requires the will and understanding that we can do more than just tread water with info business and endless self-improvement...

Small businesses, being the backbone of the economy, encounter numerous obstacles on their path to success. The main challenges include limited financial resources, lack of experience, and restricted access to advanced technologies. The concept of creating equal and sufficient conditions for the stable exchange of knowledge and experience (resources) among entrepreneurs makes sense. To achieve this, we need to use innovative technologies and methodologies aimed at supporting and developing small enterprises, providing them with the necessary tools for survival and growth.

---

7 Similar organizations that unite independent pharmacies to achieve common goals already existed in other countries. For example, in the USA, there is the National Community Pharmacists Association (NCPA), founded in 1898, which represents the interests of independent pharmacies.

The main idea is simple and not new: share successful practices and benefit from the experience of others. If someone takes a successful action, they can share it with others and receive part of their success in return. This contributes to the creation of a common pool of knowledge and expertise, allowing each market participant to effectively use the accumulated experience and gain new insights. In this way, we create an ecosystem where the success of one business becomes a resource for others.

To implement such an idea, two things are needed: methodology and technical solutions. We need a system where some people can help newcomers by sharing their knowledge and developments, thereby lifting the weaker ones and, at the same time, learning from the stronger ones.

Combining efforts and avoiding repeated "reinventions of the wheel" can lead to significant achievements, such as creating the economy of the future. The key to success here is working together on a common pool of expertise and fairly and transparently distributing investments that go into gaining experience and eliminating errors among all market participants. Thus, the market functions as a single organism, where every contribution is valuable and benefits everyone. The approach includes creating specialized support programs that consider the unique needs of each small enterprise.

Ultimately, we must strive to create a sustainable business environment where small enterprises can thrive and grow. Only through joint efforts and sharing experiences can we create a stronger and more competitive economy. Each entrepreneur, by receiving and giving, will contribute to the common cause, fostering the sustainable development of the entire market as a whole. This is the only way.

PRACTICAL EXPERIENCE AND OBSERVATIONS

In my relatively short career, I managed to work in more than three dozen companies. I often heard recommendations for my resume to stay at least a year—preferably two—in each company. However, it so happened that I simply couldn't stay in one place for that long. Sometimes financial needs forced me to change jobs, other times it was a simple lack of interest in my duties. I quickly got bored of doing the same thing, and as soon as the rules of the game became clear, I moved on. I also often didn't stay because I had no desire to play corporate political games, which are often essential for survival and career success. As a result, I can be considered a record-holder for the number of job changes. Well, "that's the way it is"… My restlessness allowed me to gain a large amount of practical experience (or "insight," as it's now trendy to say) and to understand the psychology of business through comparing different interactions with people.

With extensive business practice over time, I understood why revolutionary technological solutions are not created in companies that do not specialize in them. Besides the fact that it's simply not their business, as we've already discussed, I can confidently say that it's because of constant haste. Management sets goals, other leaders formulate tasks, and still others are in a constant rush, barely managing to deal with urgent issues. To invent and implement something new and cool, it's important to have the ability to abstract from routine and immerse oneself in a state of creativity.

Once, while working at an auto dealer company, I participated in six (!) meetings in a single day, almost all of which discussed new tasks. Of course, there was no room for creativity, and the only thing I could hope for was to carve out ten minutes during the day to grab a bite to eat. Many readers might note that there can be even more meetings in a day. There can be. But this doesn't negate the discussed problem. Operational activities and a total lack of time kill any prospects for innovation at the root.

My personal experience and the experience of even the most dedicated but employed individuals showed that in a corporate system, there is no place or time for seeking answers to philosophical questions and corresponding solutions. As we understood, this is the domain of enthusiasts inclined towards thankless and often unsuccessful experiments. Specifically, my career path helped me realize the discussed problem of small business inefficiency even in the absence of direct market demand.

The potential of the idea becomes evident when considering the already existing secondary markets in the B2C segment. People readily embrace models like second-hand stores, car swap markets, flea markets and fairs, and antique shops. These platforms have gained popularity due to two main advantages: savings and convenience. Buying used goods allows one to save a significant amount of money compared to buying new ones, which is practical in itself and especially relevant in times of economic instability.

Platforms for shared resource usage, such as BlaBlaCar, offer convenient and flexible travel solutions, making them attractive to a wide audience. Savings and convenience become key factors driving the growth and development of secondary markets.

In the quest to solve business challenges over the past decades, numerous tools have been created, most of which include various website and internet banner builders, data storage systems, widgets, and other template or ready-made solutions. Society is moving towards simplifying the means of achieving goals by creating and constantly improving various new tools. The era of neural networks has arrived, but this does not mean they will replace all the aforementioned inventions. However, like those inventions, they are designed to minimize the process of implementing our tasks and maximize the effectiveness of the results achieved.

PROSPECTS FOR IMPLEMENTING THE IDEA

Just as the world of science needs new technologies, so does the business world. The increase in the number of entrepreneurs in our time, along with trade niches and markets, has led to excessive competition in all these aspects. Consequently, the need for advertising promotion for each market participant has grown significantly, as supply now almost matches demand and even begins to exceed it. This means that someone will have to lose their market share, which we have observed in recent years. The world strives for balance, where the strongest or the smartest survive.

Of course, this likely does not apply to outstanding unique businesses, but it certainly applies to representatives of mass segments. Twenty years ago, my small hometown had only three car dealers; today, there are twenty-six, along with various trade-in centers and online services for finding the best deals, including from other regions and even countries. Supply generates demand, that's true. However, with the increase in the number of market players and the logical reduction of their market shares, the uniqueness of each in the eyes of consumers becomes diluted. Today, more than ever, you need individuality, which means positioning, image, and regular advertising. Here, I propose to consider the topic of growing associated costs.

To prepare an advertising campaign, you generally need to develop a key image, complement it with creative text, and plan where it will be shown to potential buyers. In addition to the cost of hiring a marketer to organize all this, you will need:

1. To develop an image—work of an artist (graphic designer);
2. To produce advertising media (e.g., street banners);
3. To rent advertising spaces for placing your ads.

How to reduce costs at these stages was thought of more than ten years ago and is already described above. There are buying companies that purchase advertising spaces in large volumes with corresponding discounts and then sublease them individually. The logic here is simple: buy in bulk at a lower price, lease to the end customer also at a lower price, and keep the difference.

Despite the efficiency of the model itself, the benefit for the end buyer is not as significant as it may seem. This is due to the number of intermediaries in the interaction chain, where the role of the middleman often negates the purpose of such savings due to additional bureaucracy and increased response times. After all, time is money, right? Today, we need tools that provide tangible benefits without complicating communication. For greater efficiency, something more radical in terms of business model and more direct in terms of interaction chain is required.

Secondary or shared usage might compromise the level of originality and self-identity, which today is not a significant issue. The concept of originality itself has lost relevance in the era of neural networks and such strong advertising noise, wouldn't you agree? Yes, we will have to sacrifice it, but we already do this by using constructors and other template applications like Canva, Tilda, and newer, lesser-known analogs.

A good example here is the creation of advertising materials for promotion, say, on social networks. An absolutely typical marketing task for any business, the solution to which might look like this:

1. We find like-minded individuals (this is not difficult in dealer networks, where there are hundreds of dealers with the same tasks and design standards);
2. We determine the types, formats, and advertising messages;
3. We choose a good contractor for producing materials.

And voilà! Elementary school math comes into play, showing the multiple benefits for each participant in such cooperation. Importantly, this includes the contractor, who, in addition to a good one-time volume of work, receives potential new orders in the future due to the saved advertising budgets. Thus, all participants benefit, and contributions are made to several industries — clients and contractors alike. Essentially, we reduce the average cost for each, thereby increasing the likelihood and frequency of requests to service providers. We increase the level of demand in the advertising market.

In both cases, this contributes to the survival and development of businesses without harming the participants, as they operate in different territories and have different markets. Harmony!

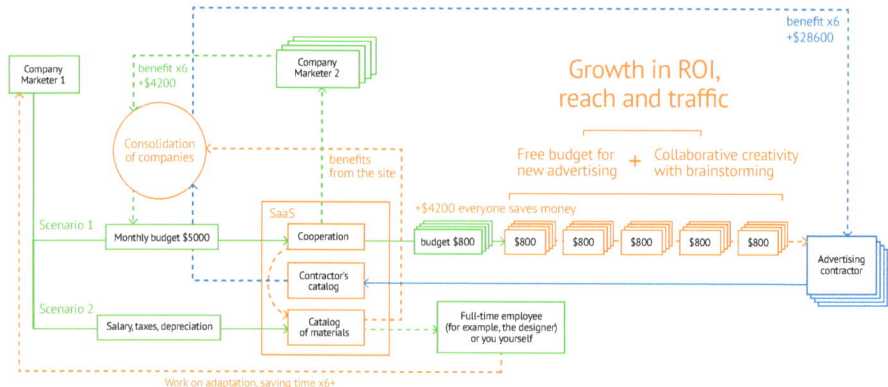

As mentioned earlier, the only condition everyone needs to be prepared for is the lack of claims to originality of the resulting product. Yes, the same advertising images will not only be yours but also used by many others. However, don't we see the same thing now with federal advertising for car brands, where dealers are forced to use identical images in their ads?

Even outside the examples of dealer networks with unified image styles, this concept has a right to exist. A small shop in Samara sells the same things as a similar shop in Vyshny Volochyok. They join forces and create a shared cool advertisement with different names and contacts, adapting it to their needs. It doesn't matter that there's a shop somewhere else with the same advertisement because it's far away, and different people, not your customers, will see it. What matters is that the advertisement is good and much more affordable than it could have been.

Analogies, in my opinion, are the simplest way to convey the idea from my perspective. In this case, I think the following comparisons are relevant.

Let's refer again to examples from B2C. In life, when people plan their budget, they often buy cars from the secondary market. The secondary market has become so popular that it surpasses the new car market by several times. But if people already have a well-established life and enough money to fully enjoy it, they are more likely to buy an expensive new car for reasons of aesthetics, healthy natural egoism, better service when buying, and the flexibility of their preferences. They want the option to choose all the settings, colors, materials, and configurations of the car because they don't need to sacrifice anything, acting to their detriment. They want service.

The same applies to marketing, in my opinion. When you are a small or just a company with many basic needs, there is no point in creating high art masterpieces and spending efforts, money, and time on it. Your strategy is to quickly create hypotheses, creatives, test them, conduct A/B testing, make adjustments, and constantly move without standing still. Conversely, if you are already a large company with branches, headquarters, and your own research centers, you invent, impress, and inspire your target audiences and even competitors, patent all your trademarks and ideas, and change trends because you already have the resources for it, you realize it and want to engage in creativity. Because the survival stage is behind you. You create.

All I want to say is that marketing is merely a matter of the company's life stage. If you are still growing, take and use ready-made solutions without worrying about ideological concerns.

> **Marketing is a matter of the company's life stage**

DEVELOPMENT OF A SAAS SOLUTION

As the reader has probably already understood, I propose considering a methodology that allows obtaining the necessary resources from a certain environment. In the case of business, this environment is the community. This means we could receive support from each other, from ourselves. People successfully use this principle in B2C on secondary markets, as we discussed earlier. In B2B, this can also work through exchange and joint cooperations.

We have the power to solve three problems at once: re-monetizing already used resources (a solution based on the principle of zero-waste production and rational use of creative power), providing a convenient, quick, and most importantly, free search for new solutions, and collective thinking when planning and creating something new.

Let's compare the concept with something simpler. In childhood, we traded toys with friends, such as robots and cars. In my case, a bit later, it was popular to exchange discs (and even cartridges) from gaming consoles. This was a must-have since few could boast about their wealth and large collections of video games in those years. These initiatives eventually led to the emergence of industry giants — platforms like Steam, GOG Galaxy, and Epic Games Store.

This is what the main gaming market in the country looked like in the 90s

Our ancestors also acted collectively. My grandfather had a cart that he sometimes lent to others, and he would occasionally borrow the collective farm's horse. We had our own small farm with cows, pigs, and chickens, but it was impossible to have everything, so we had to trade. Simple symbiosis: you help me, I help you.

Back then, this was not just a hobby or a life hack, but a necessity of life. A way to survive and feed our families. Bartering has been an effective tool since the earliest times, even before the first money appeared.

This is what my grandfather's cart looked like in the 90s, and the author (on the left in the photo)

Speaking of the solution, I mean the same thing. I am talking about creating a software solution that addresses the demands for reuse and teamwork among interested parties.

In terms of real actions, business today largely exists in isolation. The most we engage in are business breakfasts and entrepreneur clubs, where there is little practical benefit in terms of concrete actions.

I believe we can implement the concept I described above, and to prove this, I want to share my developments on this topic. Since 2019, this idea has been growing in my mind, occasionally taking shape as draft sketches and various calculations. At the time of writing this text, our team is working on a prototype of the first PRM system[8] of its kind, designed to solve the problem of resource search in the small and medium business segments. Allow me to share some details with you.

As I see it, the main problem in creating a software solution for this task is the presence of an independent party acting as an arbiter, who maintains a balance of fairness and serves as a guarantor in disputed situations. Additionally, a wide range of functionality and well-thought-out tools for its implementation are necessary. In other words, it all comes down to a well-designed service operation mechanism and a system of balances.

Draft version of the interface during the development of mechanics, 2020

---

8 Partner Relationship Management (PRM) is a system and strategy for managing relationships with partners. PRM includes methods and tools that help companies effectively interact and collaborate with their business partners, as well as create partner networks.

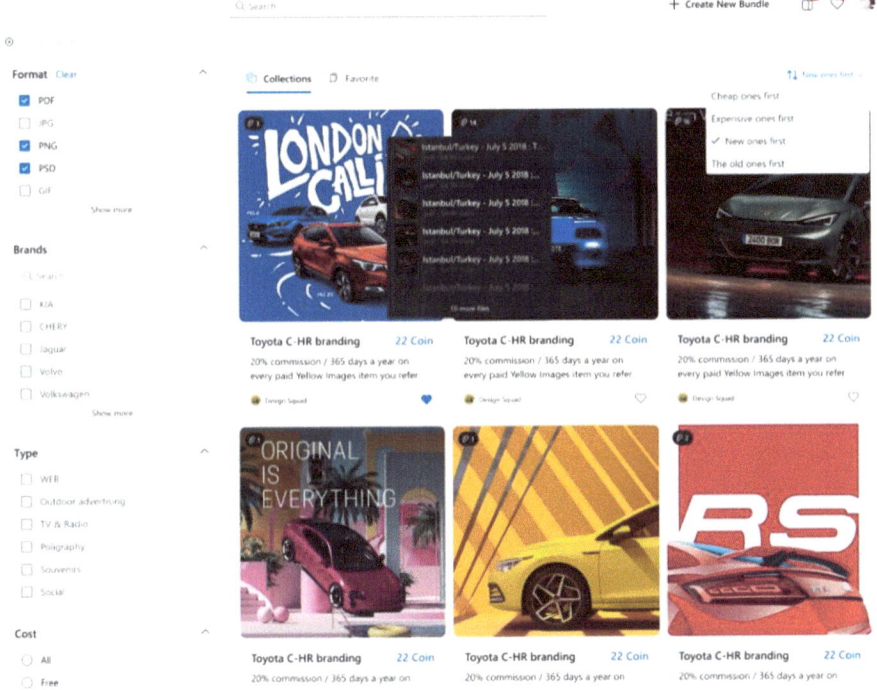

Preliminary version of the interface, 2024

As can be seen from the information above, the project underwent a long development period during which it was questioned, changed (there were at least three intermediate versions between the first and final designs), and new useful services were developed. As a result, the idea stood the test of time and began to gradually come to life. During this time, I discussed it with various people, both from the industry and outside of it. I collected feedback from car dealers and conducted surveys to gauge the potential demand for this product.

At that time, I managed to get only a few responses, but the result was quite clear:

27

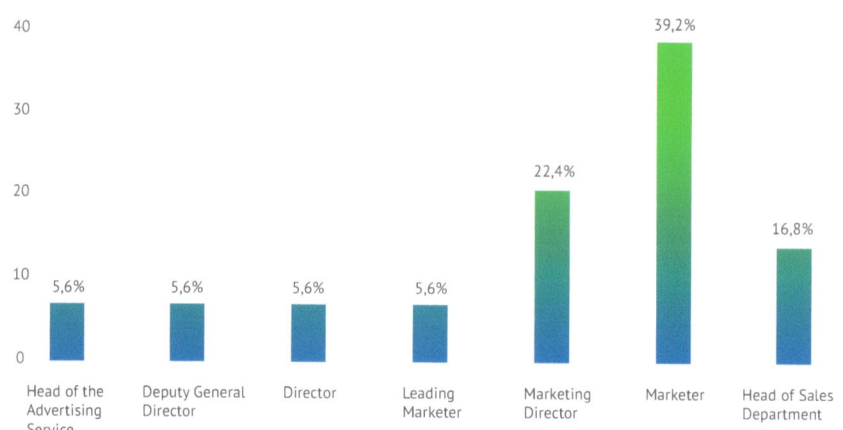

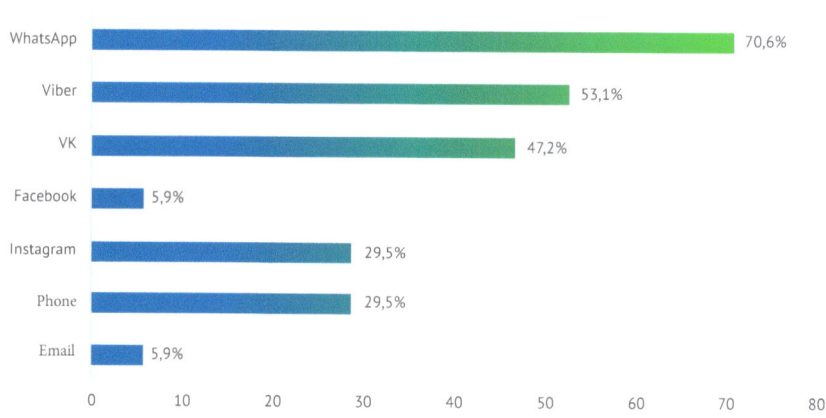

Would you be interested in the "Informational Reason" service, which is a calendar with an indication of common holidays and specially created occasions?

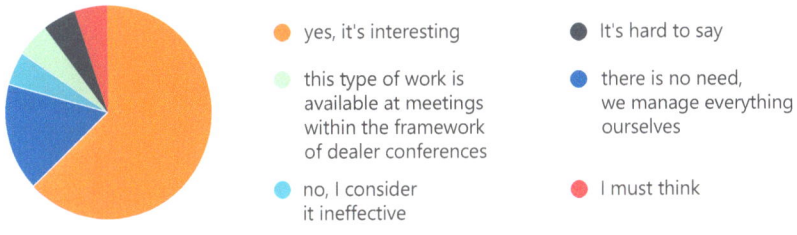

- yes, it's interesting
- this type of work is available at meetings within the framework of dealer conferences
- no, I consider it ineffective
- It's hard to say
- there is no need, we manage everything ourselves
- I must think

Would you be interested in the "Research Exchange" service, which is a list of topics on which dealers conduct external research regardless of brands and regions?

- yes, it's interesting
- there is no need, we manage everything ourselves
- I doubt the usefulness
- no, I consider it ineffective
- dealers of the region? dealers of a certain network?
- no

Would you be interested in the "Layout Sharing" service?

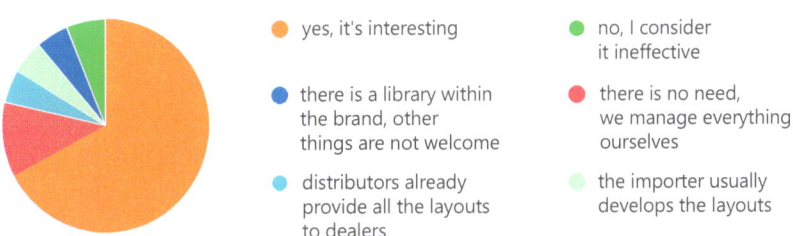

- yes, it's interesting
- there is a library within the brand, other things are not welcome
- distributors already provide all the layouts to dealers
- no, I consider it ineffective
- there is no need, we manage everything ourselves
- the importer usually develops the layouts

As can be seen from the charts, a significant portion of the audience is interested in the new solution. Some people probably didn't understand the essence of the proposed tools, thinking it was an analog of something already existing. This is not surprising, as it often happens — new wrappers for already functioning products are regularly created. For example, there are currently more than 600 CRM systems, the vast majority of which do exactly the same thing. More than six hundred, Carl!

I am confident that once the initial excitement from the effect of the working product sets in, even those who categorically refused in our survey will reconsider their opinions. In business, if you don't use it, others will.

I discussed this idea with colleagues abroad as well — marketing and sales managers, commercial directors, and even CEOs from the automotive industry, as well as advertising sales specialists with over 20 years of experience. They found it complex but interesting. The main doubts expressed were about the difficulty of reaching agreements in the case of collective development by teams with identical roles (I think this is precisely why such services have not yet been created specifically in the field of advertising).

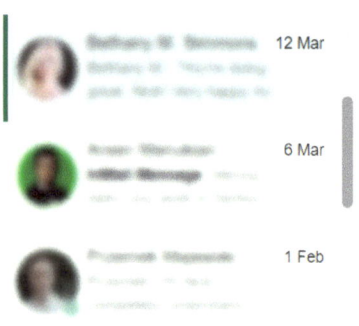

LinkedIn Correspondence

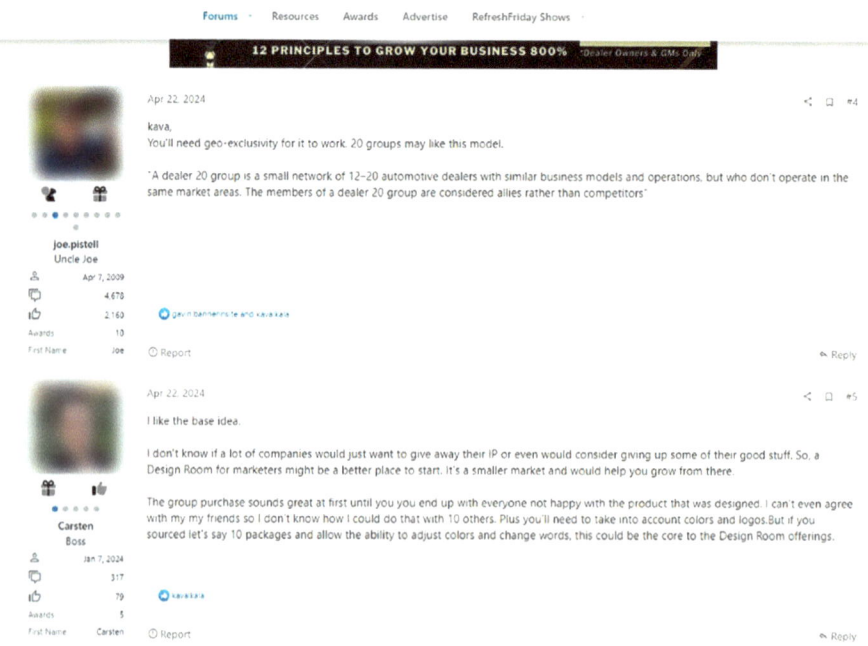

Forum Correspondence

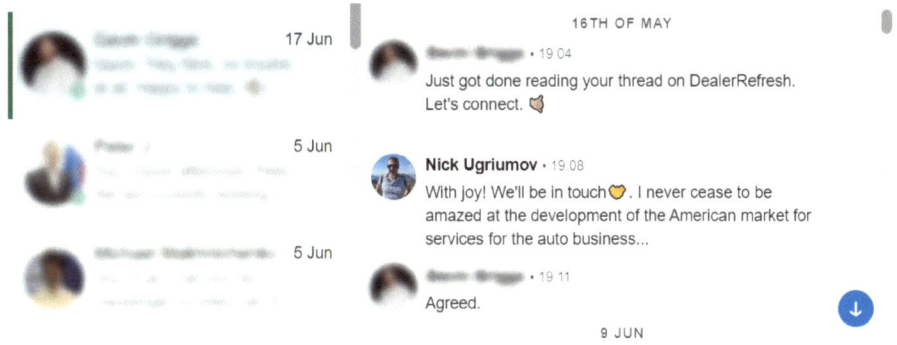

Interested contacts started emerging based on this topic

The doubts of the respondents were quite expected and understandable. We took their concerns into account during the planning stage and specifically addressed the possibilities of minimizing the risks of users receiving unexpected results. We considered this at both the management and interface mechanics levels, meticulously working through various scenarios. The mutually beneficial exchange and collaboration will allow system users to significantly:

- Accelerate the promotion creation process;
- Improve the quality of advertising materials;
- Save budget funds;
- Plan promotions more effectively.

In essence, within a brand, this could be done by the distributor (vendor), but they do not do it or do not do enough because, overall, they are indifferent—sales and associated problems are the dealers' tasks. As a result, dealers are forced to promote themselves, create image materials, and spend their own money and time on this, which is scarce in an aggressive and highly competitive business environment.

The product we are discussing will provide dealers with crowdsourcing tools, unite them even beyond specific brands and industries, and create a full-fledged business community not only based on interests but also on real interactions. To bring it to life, a fair assessment system (PRM) was carefully thought out.

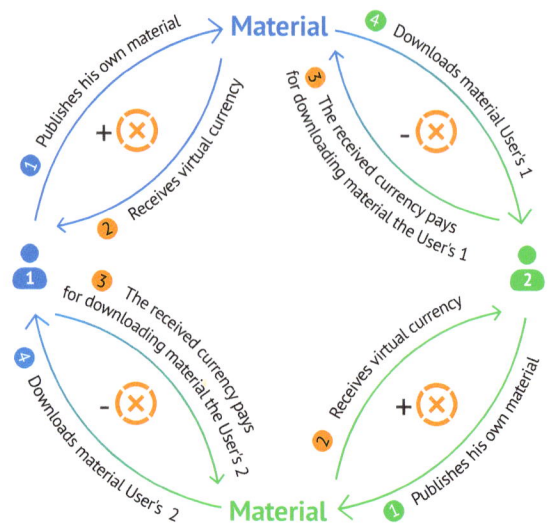

Service operation scheme: "Exchange of materials"

The logic of joint development was also carefully thought out.

Service operation scheme: "Cooperations"

In addition to their concerns about the complexities of such cooperations, my foreign colleagues expressed confidence in the benefits of the services for groups of 20 (as these groups of car dealers are informally allied with each other in the West for mutual benefit and to solve common problems). Their comments only strengthened my belief in the project.

I expect the project to benefit everyone on a win-win principle. Just take a look at the following table of advantages:

ADVANTAGES	BENEFICIARIES		
	BUSINESS	A COUNTRY	CONSUMER
The project will enable businesses to increase profitability by saving costs and boosting sales conversion. [9]	✓		
In turn, globally, this will lead to:			
• a general increase in the number of entrepreneurs due to more favorable conditions for small business development		✓	
• growth and stability of the economy in the small and medium business sectors		✓	
• the freeing up of specialists' time from unnecessary routine tasks, allowing them to focus on strategic tasks or a greater number of tactical tasks	✓		
• increased competition among car dealers, economic growth, and consequently, a reduction in retail prices in the automotive and other industries			✓
The project will enable contractors to gain access to large orders and a pool of interns, providing an incentive for the development of their business in B2B, the emergence of new market players, and the improvement of service quality.	✓		
In turn, globally, this will lead to:			
• an increase in the number of businesses in the advertising contractor sector, and consequently, the development of the advertising, design, marketing, and IT industries as a whole		✓	
• an increase in the number of jobs in society and the establishment of novice specialists in their niches			✓
• an improvement in quality of life as a result of economic growth.			✓
In summary:	3	3	3

---

[9] One of the services will be focused on increasing dealers' sales and inventory turnover.

With a final score of 3:3:3, everyone emerges as a winner. Thanks to the principle of interconnection, all market participants, including consumers, benefit in the medium and long term.

Thus, the solution addresses all the above-mentioned issues simultaneously. Moreover, it partially resolves them through each other. Using Euler circles, this logic can be visually understood. At the intersections on each side, there are zones of interest capable of generating new opportunities, development, and technologies.

The project will be a SaaS[10] system operating on the BPaaS[11] principle. We have decomposed the workflows and created functionality based on their components that allows for a significant increase in both individual and collective efficiency. According to our calculations, this efficiency can increase by 2 to 10 times depending on the specific case, with average results of 5-7 times. By using the term "efficiency," we mean saving time and money, in addition to which users will also save their energy and creative potential reserves. In my opinion, if we manage to implement the concept and engage small businesses, starting with dealer networks, the economic changes will not take long to manifest, and with the necessary scale, they will positively impact the economy of any country.

---

10 SaaS (Software as a Service) is a model for delivering software where applications are hosted on remote servers and provided to users over the internet.

11 BPaaS (Business Process as a Service) is a model for delivering business processes as a service through cloud technologies. BPaaS includes the automation and outsourcing of business processes such as accounting, human resource management, payment processing, and others, using cloud services.

CONCLUSION

In conclusion, I would like to add that if such a tool had existed during my years of working with numerous urgent tasks, I probably would have found free time for creativity... Today, marketers and entrepreneurs simply don't find the time for truly necessary tasks, getting bogged down in the specifics of promotion and operational routine—processes that truly deserve automation and simplification. True creativity should lie in improving interaction models and strategizing, not in the process of reinventing the wheel. Unfortunately or fortunately, almost all brilliant ideas have already been invented by someone. What truly amazes today is the ability to use these inventions, improve them, and move forward to new ideas without standing still. To make discoveries, revolutions, and breakthroughs.

I believe the project's concept aligns with modern approaches to achieving technological leaps, as it is rooted in the idea of uniting the efforts of the entire community. As Genghis Khan said, "One finger cannot break a stick, but five fingers, clenched into a fist, can break it easily." Just as the best engineers today are achieving humanity's transition to renewable energy, we have the power to try to save small businesses using the same principle. It is within our power and interest to create a cohesive working system, as many well-known organizations have done within specific niche demands, just as society has been doing for many years in commercial segments.

In business, it is customary to view each other as competitors because business is often compared to sports, and sports are about competition. It is time to view each other as allies and act as a single organism interested in its own prosperity. The more competitive the market, the healthier it is and the more motivated it is for new achievements.

www.ingramcontent.com/pod-product-compliance
Lightning Source LLC
Chambersburg PA
CBHW040342220526
45473CB00009B/2763